W0259688

Cram101 Textbook Outlines to accompany:

Distributed Computing: Principles, Algorithms, and Systems

Ajay D. Kshemkalyani, 1st Edition

A Content Technologies Inc. publication (c) 2012.

WHY STOP HERE... THERE'S MORE ONLINE

With technology and experience, we've developed tools that make studying easier and efficient. Like this Craml0l textbook notebook, **Craml0l.com** offers you the highlights from every chapter of your actual textbook. However, unlike this notebook, **Craml0l.com** gives you practice tests for each of the chapters. You also get access to in-depth reference material for writing essays and papers.

By purchasing this book, you get 50% off the normal subscription free!. Just enter the promotional code 'DK73DW12430' on the Cram101.com registration screen.

CRAMI0I.COM FEATURES:

Outlines & Highlights
Just like the ones in this notebook, but with links to additional information.

Integrated Note Taking
Add your class notes to the Cram101 notes, print them and maximize your study time.

Problem Solving
Step-by-step walk throughs for math, stats and other disciplines.

Practice Exams
Five different test taking formats for every chapter.

Easy Access
Study any of your books, on any computer, anywhere.

Unlimited Textbooks
All the features above for virtually all your textbooks, just add them to your account at no additional cost.

TRY THE FIRST CHAPTER FREE!

Be sure to use the promo code above when registering on Craml0l.com to get 50% off your membership fees.

STUDYING MADE EASY

This Craml0l notebook is designed to make studying easier and increase your comprehension of the textbook material. Instead of starting with a blank notebook and trying to write down everything discussed in class lectures, you can use this Craml0l textbook notebook and annotate your notes along with the lecture.

Our goal is to give you the best tools for success.

For a supreme understanding of the course, pair your notebook with our online tools. Should you decide you prefer Craml0l.com as your study tool,

we'd like to offer you a trade...

Our Trade In program is a simple way for us to keep our promise and provide you the best studying tools, regardless of where you purchased your Craml0l textbook notebook. As long as your notebook is in *Like New Condition**, you can send it back to us and we will immediately give you a Craml0l.com account free for 120 days!

Let The **Trade In** *Begin!*

THREE SIMPLE STEPS TO TRADE:

1. Go to www.cram101.com/tradein and fill out the packing slip information.
2. Submit and print the packing slip and mail it in with your Craml0l textbook notebook.
3. Activate your account after you receive your email confirmation.

* Books must be returned in *Like New Condition*, meaning there is no damage to the book including, but not limited to; ripped or torn pages, markings or writing on pages, or folded / creased pages. Upon receiving the book, Craml0l will inspect it and reserves the right to terminate your free Craml0l.com account and return your textbook notebook at the owners expense.

Learning System

Cram101 Textbook Outlines is a learning system. The notes in this book are the highlights of your textbook, you will never have to highlight a book again.

How to use this book. Take this book to class, it is your notebook for the lecture. The notes and highlights on the left hand side of the pages follow the outline and order of the textbook. All you have to do is follow along while your instructor presents the lecture. Circle the items emphasized in class and add other important information on the right side. With Cram101 Textbook Outlines you'll spend less time writing and more time listening. Learning becomes more efficient.

Cram101.com Online

Increase your studying efficiency by using Cram101.com's practice tests and online reference material. It is the perfect complement to Cram101 Textbook Outlines. Use self-teaching matching tests or simulate in-class testing with comprehensive multiple choice tests, or simply use Cram's true and false tests for quick review. Cram101.com even allows you to enter your in-class notes for an integrated studying format combining the textbook notes with your class notes.

Visit **www.Cram101.com**, click Sign Up at the top of the screen, and enter **DK73DW12430** in the promo code box on the registration screen. Your access to www.Cram101.com is discounted by 50% because you have purchased this book. Sign up and stop highlighting textbooks forever.

 ISBN(s): 9781614902980. PUBR-6.201153

Distributed Computing: Principles, Algorithms, and Systems
Ajay D. Kshemkalyani, 1st

CONTENTS

Chapter 1. Introduction

Otway-Rees protocol	The Otway-Rees protocol is a computer network authentication protocol designed for use on insecure networks (eg. the Internet). It allows individuals communicating over such a network to prove their identity to each other while also preventing eavesdropping or replay attacks and allowing for the detection of modification.
Protocol	In object-oriented programming, a protocol is what or how unrelated objects use to communicate with each other. These are definitions of methods and values which the objects agree upon in order to cooperate. For example, in Java (where protocols are termed interfaces), the `Comparable` interface specifies a method `compareTo` which implementing classes should implement.
Taxonomy	Taxonomy is the practice and science of classification. The word finds its roots in the Greek τ?ξις, taxis (meaning 'order' or 'arrangement') and ν?μος, nomos (meaning 'law' or 'science'). Taxonomy uses taxonomic units, known as taxa .
Interconnection	In telecommunications, interconnection is the physical linking of a carrier's network with equipment or facilities not belonging to that network. The term may refer to a connection between a carrier's facilities and the equipment belonging to its customer, or to a connection between two (or more) carriers. In United States regulatory law, interconnection is specifically defined (47 C.F.R. 51.5) as "the linking of two networks for the mutual exchange of traffic." One of the primary tools used by regulators to introduce competition in telecommunications markets has been to impose interconnection requirements on dominant carriers.
Coupling	In electronics and telecommunication, coupling is the desirable or undesirable transfer of energy from one medium, such as a metallic wire or an optical fiber, to another medium, including fortuitous transfer.

Coupling is also the transfer of electrical energy from one circuit segment to another. For example, energy is transferred from a power source to an electrical load by means of conductive coupling, which may be either resistive or hard-wire. An AC potential may be transferred from one circuit segment to another having a DC potential by use of a capacitor. Electrical energy may be transferred from one circuit segmant to another segment with different impedance by use of a transformer.

Internet

The Internet is a global system of interconnected computer networks that use the standard Internet Protocol Suite (TCP/IP) to serve billions of users worldwide. It is a network of networks that consists of millions of private, public, academic, business, and government networks, of local to global scope, that are linked by a broad array of electronic, wireless and optical networking technologies. The Internet carries a vast range of information resources and services, such as the inter-linked hypertext documents of the World Wide Web (WWW) and the infrastructure to support electronic mail.

Concurrency

In computer science, concurrency is a property of systems in which several computations are executing simultaneously, and potentially interacting with each other. The computations may be executing on multiple cores in the same chip, preemptively time-shared threads on the same processor, or executed on physically separated processors. A number of mathematical models have been developed for general concurrent computation including Petri nets, process calculi, the Parallel Random Access Machine model and the Actor model.

EPSILON

A macro language with high level features including strings and lists, developed by A.P. Ershov at Novosibirsk in 1967. EPSILON was used to implement ALGOL 68 on the M-220 computer.

Shared memory

In computing, shared memory is memory that may be simultaneously accessed by multiple programs with an intent to provide communication among them or avoid redundant copies. Depending on context, programs may run on a single processor or on multiple separate processors. Using memory for communication inside a single program, for example among its multiple threads, is generally not referred to as shared memory.

Blocking

Blocking occurs when a function does not return until it either completes its task or results in an error.

A process that is blocked is one that waits for the completion of some event, such as an I/O operation

In a hypothetical two state model (running and not-running), processes would go onto the (running) queue before being dispatched for execution. In the absence of a blocked state, if priority is measured by holdup time, blocked processes would erroneously get scheduled despite having nothing to operate on.

Tapestry

Tapestry is a distributed hash table which provides a decentralized object location, routing, and multicasting infrastructure for distributed applications. It is composed of a peer-to-peer overlay network offering efficient, scalable, self-repairing, location-aware routing to nearby resources.

The first generation of peer-to-peer applications, including Napster, Gnutella, had restricting limitations such as a central directory for Napster and scoped broadcast queries for Gnutella limiting scalability.

Algorithm

In mathematics and computer science, an algorithm is an effective method expressed as a finite list of well-defined instructions for calculating a function. Algorithms are used for calculation, data processing, and automated reasoning.

Starting from an initial state and initial input (perhaps null), the instructions describe a computation that, when executed, will proceed through a finite number of well-defined successive states, eventually producing "output" and terminating at a final ending state.

Relation

In relational model:

A relation is a data structure which consists of a heading and an unordered set of tuples which share the same type.

When Edgar F. Codd invented the relational model, he generalized the concept of binary relation to n-ary relation. Relation is a fundamental concept in relational model.

A relation has zero or more tuples.

A relation value is an instance of a relation.

A relation variable (relvar) is a variable which has a relation value.

In some context, relation means relation variable.

State

In computer science and automata theory, a state is a unique configuration of information in a program or machine. It is a concept that occasionally extends into some forms of systems programming such as lexers and parsers.

Whether the automaton in question is a finite state machine, a pushdown automaton or a full-fledged Turing machine, a state is a particular set of instructions which will be executed in response to the machine's input.

Snapshot

In computer systems, a snapshot is the state of a system at a particular point in time. The term was coined as an analogy to that in photography. It can refer to an actual copy of the state of a system or to a capability provided by certain systems.

State

In computer science and automata theory, a state is a unique configuration of information in a program or machine. It is a concept that occasionally extends into some forms of systems programming such as lexers and parsers.

Whether the automaton in question is a finite state machine, a pushdown automaton or a full-fledged Turing machine, a state is a particular set of instructions which will be executed in response to the machine's input.

Computation

Computation is a general term for any type of process, algorithm or measurement; this often includes but is not limited to digital data. This includes phenomena ranging from human thinking to calculations with a more narrow meaning. Computation is a process following a well-defined model that is understood and can be expressed in an algorithm, protocol, network topology, etc.

Event

In computing an event is an action that is usually initiated outside the scope of a program and that is handled by a piece of code inside the program. Typically events are handled synchronous with the program flow, that is, the program has one or more dedicated places where events are handled. Typical sources of events include the user (who presses a key on the keyboard, in other words, through a keystroke).

EPSILON

A macro language with high level features including strings and lists, developed by A.P. Ershov at Novosibirsk in 1967. EPSILON was used to implement ALGOL 68 on the M-220 computer.

Chapter 3. Logical time

Internet

The Internet is a global system of interconnected computer networks that use the standard Internet Protocol Suite (TCP/IP) to serve billions of users worldwide. It is a network of networks that consists of millions of private, public, academic, business, and government networks, of local to global scope, that are linked by a broad array of electronic, wireless and optical networking technologies. The Internet carries a vast range of information resources and services, such as the inter-linked hypertext documents of the World Wide Web (WWW) and the infrastructure to support electronic mail.

Concurrency

In computer science, concurrency is a property of systems in which several computations are executing simultaneously, and potentially interacting with each other. The computations may be executing on multiple cores in the same chip, preemptively time-shared threads on the same processor, or executed on physically separated processors. A number of mathematical models have been developed for general concurrent computation including Petri nets, process calculi, the Parallel Random Access Machine model and the Actor model.

Logical clock

A logical clock is a mechanism for capturing chronological and causal relationships in a distributed system.

Logical clock algorithms of note are:

- Lamport timestamps, which are monotonically increasing software counters.
- Vector clocks, that allow for total ordering of events in a distributed system.
- Version vectors, order replicas, according to updates, in an optimistic replicated system.
- Matrix clocks, an extension of vector clocks that also contains information about other processes' views of the system.

.

Chord

A chord is a concurrency construct available in Polyphonic C? and Cω inspired by the join pattern of the join-calculus.

Synchronicity

Cω defines two types of functions synchronous and asynchronous. A synchronous function acts like a standard function in most Object-Oriented Language, upon invocation the function body is executed and a return value may or may not be returned to the caller.

Tapestry	Tapestry is a distributed hash table which provides a decentralized object location, routing, and multicasting infrastructure for distributed applications. It is composed of a peer-to-peer overlay network offering efficient, scalable, self-repairing, location-aware routing to nearby resources. The first generation of peer-to-peer applications, including Napster, Gnutella, had restricting limitations such as a central directory for Napster and scoped broadcast queries for Gnutella limiting scalability.
Scalar	In computing, a scalar variable or field is one that can hold only one value at a time; as opposed to composite variables like array, list, hash, record, etc. In some contexts, a scalar value may be understood to be numeric. A scalar data type is the type of a scalar variable.
Counting	Counting is the mathematical action of continually adding (or subtracting) one at a time, usually to find out how many objects there are or to set aside a desired number of objects , to find the ordinal number of a particular object, or to find the object with a particular ordinal number. counting is also used (primarily by children) to demonstrate knowledge of the number names and the number system. Sometimes the term counting is used to mean the same as enumeration, i.e. finding the number of elements of a finite set).
Event	In computing an event is an action that is usually initiated outside the scope of a program and that is handled by a piece of code inside the program. Typically events are handled synchronous with the program flow, that is, the program has one or more dedicated places where events are handled. Typical sources of events include the user (who presses a key on the keyboard, in other words, through a keystroke).
Protocol	In object-oriented programming, a protocol is what or how unrelated objects use to communicate with each other. These are definitions of methods and values which the objects agree upon in order to cooperate. For example, in Java (where protocols are termed interfaces), the `Comparable` interface specifies a method `compareTo` which implementing classes should implement.

Vector

A vector in computing, specifically when talking about malicious code such as viruses or worms, is the method that this code uses to propagate itself or infect the computer and this sense is similar to, and derived from, its meaning in biology.

Some common vectors:

- buffer overflows -- this is how the Blaster worm was able to propagate
- HTML email with JavaScript or other scripting enhancements
- networking protocol flaws

Vector clock

Vector clocks is an algorithm for generating a partial ordering of events in a distributed system and detecting causality violations. Just as in Lamport timestamps, interprocess messages contain the state of the sending process's logical clock. A vector clock of a system of N processes is an array/vector of N logical clocks, one clock per process; a local "smallest possible values" copy of the global clock-array is kept in each process, with the following rules for clock updates:

- Initially all clocks are zero.
- Each time a process experiences an internal event, it increments its own logical clock in the vector by one.
- Each time a process prepares to send a message, it increments its own logical clock in the vector by one and then sends its entire vector along with the message being sent.
- Each time a process receives a message, it increments its own logical clock in the vector by one and updates each element in its vector by taking the maximum of the value in its own vector clock and the value in the vector in the received message (for every element).

The vector clocks algorithm was independently developed by Colin Fidge and Friedemann Mattern in 1988.

Partial ordering property

Vector clocks allow for the partial causal ordering of events.

Size

Size is a command line utility originally written for use with the Unix-like operating systems. It processes one or more ELF files and its output are the dimensions (in bytes) of the text, data and uninitialized sections, and their total.

Common use:

$ size ...

Here follows some examples on Solaris (/usr/ccs/bin/size); options and syntax may vary on different Operating Systems:

$ size /usr/ccs/bin/size9066 + 888 + 356 = 10310

With -f option name and size of each section are printed out, plus their total:

$ size -f /usr/ccs/bin/size17(.interp) + 636(.hash) + 1440(.dynsym) + 743(.dynstr) + 64 (.SUNW_version) + 48(.rela.ex_shared) + 24(.rela.bss) + 336(.rela.plt) + 4760(.text) +80(.init) + 80(.fini) + 4(.exception_ranges) + 28(.rodata) + 590(.rodata1) + 12(.got) + 388(.plt) + 192 (.dynamic) + 40(.ex_shared) + 112(.data) +140(.data1) + 352(.bss) = 10086

With -F option size and permission flag of each sections are printed out, plus their total:

$ size -F /usr/ccs/bin/size9066(r-x) + 1244(rwx) = 10470

.

Implementation	Implementation is the realization of an application, idea, model, design, specification, standard, algorithm, or policy. In computer science, an implementation(computer science) · Programming language implementation · Algorithm · Application software · Code · Computation · Function · Method · Process · Proceeding · Procedure · Scheme · Solution · System · Technique '.
Matrix	In hot metal typesetting, a matrix is a mold for casting the letters known as sorts used in letterpress printing.

In letterpress typography the matrix of one letter is inserted into the bottom of a hand mould, the mould is locked and molten type metal is poured into a straight-sided vertical cavity above the matrix. When the metal has cooled and solidified the mould is unlocked and a newly-cast metal sort is removed, ready for composition with other sorts.

Matrix clocks

A matrix clock is a mechanism for capturing chronological and causal relationships in a distributed system.

Matrix clocks are a generalization of the notion of vector clocks. A matrix clock maintains a vector of the vector clocks for each communicating host.

Virtual

The word virtual has been applied to computing and information technology with various meanings.

It is used of software systems that act as if they were hardware systems (virtual machine, virtual memory, virtual disk), of computer-generated simulations of reality (virtual reality), and of internet gaming environments wherein entire worlds are created (virtual world) or the real world is supplemented with virtual images (augmented reality). Other applications of the word are being found constantly in this fast expanding field, such as virtual community, virtual library, and virtual class.

Clock synchronization

Clock synchronization is a problem from computer science and engineering which deals with the idea that internal clocks of several computers may differ. Even when initially set accurately, real clocks will differ after some amount of time due to clock drift, caused by clocks counting time at slightly different rates. There are several problems that occur as a repercussion of rate differences and several solutions, some being more appropriate than others in certain contexts.

Synchronization

In computer science, synchronization refers to one of two distinct but related concepts: synchronization of processes, and synchronization of data. Process synchronization refers to the idea that multiple processes are to join up or handshake at a certain point, so as to reach an agreement or commit to a certain sequence of action. Data synchronization refers to the idea of keeping multiple copies of a dataset in coherence with one another, or to maintain data integrity.

Offset

In computer science, an offset within an array or other data structure object is an integer indicating the distance (displacement) from the beginning of the object up until a given element or point, presumably within the same object. The concept of a distance is valid only if all elements of the object are the same size (typically given in bytes or words).

For example, given an array of characters A, containing `abcdef`, one can say that the element containing the letter '`c`' has an offset of 2 from the start of A.

In computer engineering and low-level programming (such as assembly language), an offset usually denotes the number of address locations added to a base address in order to get to a specific absolute address.

Network Time Protocol

The Network Time Protocol is a protocol for synchronizing the clocks of computer systems over packet-switched, variable-latency data networks. It is designed particularly to resist the effects of variable latency by using a jitter buffer.

Network Time Protocol is one of the oldest Internet protocols still in use (since before 1985).

Time Protocol

The Time Protocol is a network protocol in the Internet Protocol Suite defined in 1983 in RFC 868. Its purpose is to provide a site-independent, machine readable date and time.

The Time Protocol may be implemented over the Transmission Control Protocol (TCP) or the User Datagram Protocol (UDP). A host connects to a server that supports the Time Protocol on port 37. The server then sends the time as a 32-bit unsigned integer in binary format and in network byte order, representing the number of seconds since 00:00 (midnight) 1 January, 1900 GMT, and closes the connection.

Internet

The Internet is a global system of interconnected computer networks that use the standard Internet Protocol Suite (TCP/IP) to serve billions of users worldwide. It is a network of networks that consists of millions of private, public, academic, business, and government networks, of local to global scope, that are linked by a broad array of electronic, wireless and optical networking technologies. The Internet carries a vast range of information resources and services, such as the inter-linked hypertext documents of the World Wide Web (WWW) and the infrastructure to support electronic mail.

Snapshot

In computer systems, a snapshot is the state of a system at a particular point in time. The term was coined as an analogy to that in photography. It can refer to an actual copy of the state of a system or to a capability provided by certain systems.

State

In computer science and automata theory, a state is a unique configuration of information in a program or machine. It is a concept that occasionally extends into some forms of systems programming such as lexers and parsers.

Whether the automaton in question is a finite state machine, a pushdown automaton or a full-fledged Turing machine, a state is a particular set of instructions which will be executed in response to the machine's input.

Protocol

In object-oriented programming, a protocol is what or how unrelated objects use to communicate with each other. These are definitions of methods and values which the objects agree upon in order to cooperate.

For example, in Java (where protocols are termed interfaces), the `Comparable` interface specifies a method `compareTo` which implementing classes should implement.

Property

A property, in some object-oriented programming languages, is a special sort of class member, intermediate between a field (or data member) and a method. Properties are read and written like fields, but property reads and writes are (usually) translated to get and set method calls. The field-like syntax is said to be easier to read and write than lots of method calls, yet the interposition of method calls allows for data validation, active updating (as of GUI visuals), and/or read-only 'fields'.

Channel

Color digital images are made of pixels, and pixels are made of combinations of primary colors. A channel in this context is the grayscale image of the same size as a color image, made of just one of these primary colors. For instance, an image from a standard digital camera will have a red, green and blue channel.

Password

A password is a secret word or string of characters that is used for authentication, to prove identity or gain access to a resource (example: an access code is a type of password). The password should be kept secret from those not allowed access.

The use of passwords is known to be ancient.

Condition

A relational database management system uses SQL conditions or expressions in `WHERE` clauses and in `HAVING` clauses to `SELECT` subsets of data.

Types of condition

- Many conditions compare values for (for example) equality, inequality or similarity.
- The EXISTS condition uses the SQL standard keyword `EXISTS` to determine whether rows exist in a subquery result.

Examples

To `SELECT` one row of data from a table called tab with a primary key column (pk) set to 100 -- use the condition pk = 100:

```
SELECT * FROM tab WHERE pk = 100
```

To identify whether a table tab has rows of data with a duplicated key column dk set to 100 -- use the condition dk = 100 and the condition having count(*) > 1:

SELECT * FROM tab WHERE dk = 100 having count(*) > 1

.

Algorithm

In mathematics and computer science, an algorithm is an effective method expressed as a finite list of well-defined instructions for calculating a function. Algorithms are used for calculation, data processing, and automated reasoning.

Starting from an initial state and initial input (perhaps null), the instructions describe a computation that, when executed, will proceed through a finite number of well-defined successive states, eventually producing "output" and terminating at a final ending state.

Otway-Rees protocol	The Otway-Rees protocol is a computer network authentication protocol designed for use on insecure networks (eg. the Internet). It allows individuals communicating over such a network to prove their identity to each other while also preventing eavesdropping or replay attacks and allowing for the detection of modification.
Protocol	In object-oriented programming, a protocol is what or how unrelated objects use to communicate with each other. These are definitions of methods and values which the objects agree upon in order to cooperate. For example, in Java (where protocols are termed interfaces), the `Comparable` interface specifies a method `compareTo` which implementing classes should implement.
Adaptive algorithm	An adaptive algorithm is an algorithm that changes its behavior based on the resources available. For example, stable partition, using no additional memory is O(n lg n) but given O(n) memory, it can be O(n) in time. As implemented by the C++ Standard Library, `stable_partition` is adaptive and so it acquires as much memory as it can get (up to what it would need at most) and applies the algorithm using that available memory.
Algorithm	In mathematics and computer science, an algorithm is an effective method expressed as a finite list of well-defined instructions for calculating a function. Algorithms are used for calculation, data processing, and automated reasoning. Starting from an initial state and initial input (perhaps null), the instructions describe a computation that, when executed, will proceed through a finite number of well-defined successive states, eventually producing "output" and terminating at a final ending state.
Asynchronous system	In a synchronous system, operations are coordinated under the centralized control of a fixed-rate clock signal or several clocks. An asynchronous digital system, in contrast, has no global clock: instead, it operates under distributed control, with concurrent hardware components communicating and synchronizing on channels. Modularity

Asynchronous systems -- much like object-oriented software -- are typically constructed out of modular 'hardware objects', each with well-defined communication interfaces.

Internet

The Internet is a global system of interconnected computer networks that use the standard Internet Protocol Suite (TCP/IP) to serve billions of users worldwide. It is a network of networks that consists of millions of private, public, academic, business, and government networks, of local to global scope, that are linked by a broad array of electronic, wireless and optical networking technologies. The Internet carries a vast range of information resources and services, such as the inter-linked hypertext documents of the World Wide Web (WWW) and the infrastructure to support electronic mail.

METRIC

METRIC is a computer model (Mapping EvapoTranspiration at high Resolution with Internalized Calibration) that uses Landsat satellite data to compute and map evapotranspiration (ET) developed by the University of Idaho.

Spanning tree

In the mathematical field of graph theory, a spanning tree T of a connected, undirected graph G is a tree composed of all the vertices and some (or perhaps all) of the edges of G. Informally, a spanning tree of G is a selection of edges of G that form a tree spanning every vertex. That is, every vertex lies in the tree, but no cycles (or loops) are formed. On the other hand, every bridge of G must belong to T.

A spanning tree of a connected graph G can also be defined as a maximal set of edges of G that contains no cycle, or as a minimal set of edges that connect all vertices.

Snapshot

In computer systems, a snapshot is the state of a system at a particular point in time. The term was coined as an analogy to that in photography. It can refer to an actual copy of the state of a system or to a capability provided by certain systems.

Single

In music, a single is a type of release, typically a recording of fewer tracks than an LP or a CD. This can be released for sale to the public in a variety of different formats. In most cases, the single is a song that is released separately from an album, but it can still appear on an album. Often, these are the most popular songs from albums that are released separately for promotional uses, and in other cases a recording released as a single does not appear on an album. 45 rpm records were played on a record player or turntable.

Vector

A vector in computing, specifically when talking about malicious code such as viruses or worms, is the method that this code uses to propagate itself or infect the computer and this sense is similar to, and derived from, its meaning in biology.

Some common vectors:

- buffer overflows -- this is how the Blaster worm was able to propagate
- HTML email with JavaScript or other scripting enhancements
- networking protocol flaws

PATH

PATH is an environment variable on Unix-like operating systems, DOS, OS/2, and Microsoft Windows, specifying a set of directories where executable programs are located. In general, each executing process or user session has its own PATH setting.

Unix and Unix-like

On POSIX and Unix-like operating systems, the `$PATH` variable is specified as a list of one or more directory names separated by colon (`:`) characters.

Minimum weight

In error-correcting coding, the minimum Hamming weight, commonly referred to as the minimum weight w_{min} of a code is the weight of the lowest-weight code word. The weight w of a code word is the number of 1s in the word. For example the word 11001010 has a weight of 4.

Synchronizer

In computer science, a synchronizer is an algorithm that can be used to run a synchronous algorithm on top of an asynchronous processor network, so enabling the asynchronous system to run as a synchronous network.

The concept was originally proposed in (Awerbuch, 1985) along with three synchronizer algorithms named alpha, beta and gamma which provided different tradeoffs in terms of time and message complexity. Essentially, they are a solution to the problem of asynchronous algorithms (which operate in a network with no global clock) being harder to design and often less efficient than the equivalent synchronous algorithms.

Independent set

In graph theory, an independent set is a set of vertices in a graph, no two of which are adjacent. That is, it is a set I of vertices such that for every two vertices in I, there is no edge connecting the two. Equivalently, each edge in the graph has at most one endpoint in I. The size of an independent set is the number of vertices it contains.

Maximal independent set

In graph theory, a maximal independent set is not a subset of any other independent set. That is, it is a set S such that every edge of the graph has at least one endpoint not in S and every vertex not in S has at least one neighbor in S. A maximal independent set is also a dominating set in the graph, and every dominating set that is independent must be maximal independent, so maximal independent sets are also called independent dominating sets. A graph may have many maximal independent sets of widely varying sizes; a largest maximal independent set is called a maximum independent set.

Connected dominating set

In graph theory, a connected dominated set and a maximum leaf spanning tree are two closely related structures defined on an undirected graph.

Definitions

A connected dominating set of a graph G is a set D of vertices with two properties:

1. Any node in D can reach any other node in D by a path that stays entirely within D. That is, D induces a connected subgraph of G.
2. Every vertex in G either belongs to D or is adjacent to a vertex in D. That is, D is a dominating set of G.

A minimum connected dominating set of a graph G is a connecting dominating set with the smallest possible cardinality among all connected dominating sets of G. The connected domination number of G is the number of vertices in the minimum connected dominating set.

Any spanning tree T of a graph G has at least two leaves, vertices that have only one edge of T incident to them.

Dominating set

In graph theory, a dominating set for a graph G = (V, E) is a subset D of V such that every vertex not in D is joined to at least one member of D by some edge. The domination number γ(G) is the number of vertices in a smallest dominating set for G.

The dominating set problem concerns testing whether γ(G) ≤ K for a given graph G and input K; it is a classical NP-complete decision problem in computational complexity theory (Garey ' Johnson 1979). Therefore it is believed that there is no efficient algorithm that finds a smallest dominating set for a given graph.

Routing

Routing is the process of selecting paths in a network along which to send network traffic.

Routing table

In computer networking a routing table, is a data structure in the form of a table-like object stored in a router or a networked computer that lists the routes to particular network destinations, and in some cases, metrics associated with those routes. The routing table contains information about the topology of the network immediately around it. The construction of routing tables is the primary goal of routing protocols.

Table

In relational databases and flat file databases, a table is a set of data elements (values) that is organized using a model of vertical columns (which are identified by their name) and horizontal rows. A table has a specified number of columns, but can have any number of rows. Each row is identified by the values appearing in a particular column subset which has been identified as a candidate key.

Leader election

In distributed computing, leader election is the process of designating a single process as the organizer of some task distributed among several computers (nodes). Before the task is begun, all network nodes are unaware which node will serve as the "leader," or coordinator, of the task. After a leader election algorithm has been run, however, each node throughout the network recognizes a particular, unique node as the task leader.

Replication	Replication is the process of sharing information so as to ensure consistency between redundant resources, such as software or hardware components, to improve reliability, fault-tolerance, or accessibility. It could be data replication if the same data is stored on multiple storage devices, or computation replication if the same computing task is executed many times. A computational task is typically replicated in space, i.e. executed on separate devices, or it could be replicated in time, if it is executed repeatedly on a single device.

Chapter 6. Message ordering and group communication

Order

In scientific classification used in biology, the order is

1. a taxonomic rank used in the classification of organisms. Other well-known ranks are life, domain, kingdom, phylum, class, family, genus, and species, with order fitting in between class and family. An immediately higher rank, superorder, may be added directly above order, while suborder would be a lower rank.
2. a taxonomic unit, a taxon, in that rank.

Protocol

In object-oriented programming, a protocol is what or how unrelated objects use to communicate with each other. These are definitions of methods and values which the objects agree upon in order to cooperate.

For example, in Java (where protocols are termed interfaces), the `Comparable` interface specifies a method `compareTo` which implementing classes should implement.

Snapshot

In computer systems, a snapshot is the state of a system at a particular point in time. The term was coined as an analogy to that in photography. It can refer to an actual copy of the state of a system or to a capability provided by certain systems.

Rendezvous

Rendezvous is a data synchronization mechanism in Plan 9 from Bell Labs. It is a system call that allows two processes to exchange a single data item while synchronizing.

The rendezvous call takes a tag and a value as its arguments.

Group

Group is a name service database used to store group information on Unix-like operating systems.

The sources for the group database (and hence the sources for groups on a system) are configured, like other name service databases, in nsswitch.conf.

Seeing the available groups on a Unix system

The contents of the group database (and available groups) can be seen with a variety of tools:

Command line

The getent command can be used to fetch group information.

Algorithm

In mathematics and computer science, an algorithm is an effective method expressed as a finite list of well-defined instructions for calculating a function. Algorithms are used for calculation, data processing, and automated reasoning.

Starting from an initial state and initial input (perhaps null), the instructions describe a computation that, when executed, will proceed through a finite number of well-defined successive states, eventually producing "output" and terminating at a final ending state.

Tapestry

Tapestry is a distributed hash table which provides a decentralized object location, routing, and multicasting infrastructure for distributed applications. It is composed of a peer-to-peer overlay network offering efficient, scalable, self-repairing, location-aware routing to nearby resources.

The first generation of peer-to-peer applications, including Napster, Gnutella, had restricting limitations such as a central directory for Napster and scoped broadcast queries for Gnutella limiting scalability.

Chapter 6. Message ordering and group communication

Distributed algorithms	A distributed algorithm is an algorithm designed to run on computer hardware constructed from interconnected processors. Distributed algorithms are used in many varied application areas of distributed computing, such as telecommunications, scientific computing, distributed information processing, and real-time process control. Standard problems solved by distributed algorithms include leader election, consensus, distributed search, spanning tree generation, mutual exclusion, and resource allocation.
Multicast	In computer networking, multicast is the delivery of a message or information to a group of destination computers simultaneously in a single transmission from the source creating copies automatically in other network elements, such as routers, only when the topology of the network requires it. Multicast is most commonly implemented in IP multicast, which is often employed in Internet Protocol (IP) applications of streaming media and Internet television. In IP multicast the implementation of the multicast concept occurs at the IP routing level, where routers create optimal distribution paths for datagrams sent to a multicast destination address.
Privilege	In computing, privilege is defined as the delegation of authority over a computer system. A privilege is a permission to perform an action. Examples of various privileges include the ability to create a file in a directory, or to read or delete a file, access a device, or have read or write permission to a socket for communicating over the Internet.
Core-based trees	Core-Based Trees is a proposal for making IP Multicast scalable by constructing a tree of routers. It was first proposed in a paper by Ballardie, Francis, and Crowcroft. What differentiates it from other schemes for multicasting is that the routing tree comprises multiple "cores" (also known as "centres").

Tapestry

Tapestry is a distributed hash table which provides a decentralized object location, routing, and multicasting infrastructure for distributed applications. It is composed of a peer-to-peer overlay network offering efficient, scalable, self-repairing, location-aware routing to nearby resources.

The first generation of peer-to-peer applications, including Napster, Gnutella, had restricting limitations such as a central directory for Napster and scoped broadcast queries for Gnutella limiting scalability.

Snapshot

In computer systems, a snapshot is the state of a system at a particular point in time. The term was coined as an analogy to that in photography. It can refer to an actual copy of the state of a system or to a capability provided by certain systems.

Spanning tree

In the mathematical field of graph theory, a spanning tree T of a connected, undirected graph G is a tree composed of all the vertices and some (or perhaps all) of the edges of G. Informally, a spanning tree of G is a selection of edges of G that form a tree spanning every vertex. That is, every vertex lies in the tree, but no cycles (or loops) are formed. On the other hand, every bridge of G must belong to T.

A spanning tree of a connected graph G can also be defined as a maximal set of edges of G that contains no cycle, or as a minimal set of edges that connect all vertices.

General

A general officer is an officer of very high military rank. The term or equivalent is used by nearly every country in the world. general can be used as a generic term for all grades of general officer, or it can specifically refer to a single rank that is simply called general.

Protocol

In object-oriented programming, a protocol is what or how unrelated objects use to communicate with each other. These are definitions of methods and values which the objects agree upon in order to cooperate.

For example, in Java (where protocols are termed interfaces), the `Comparable` interface specifies a method `compareTo` which implementing classes should implement.

Dynamics

In music, dynamics normally refers to the volume of a sound or note, but can also refer to every aspect of the execution of a given piece, either stylistic (staccato, legato etc). or functional (velocity). The term is also applied to the written or printed musical notation used to indicate dynamics.

Computation

Computation is a general term for any type of process, algorithm or measurement; this often includes but is not limited to digital data. This includes phenomena ranging from human thinking to calculations with a more narrow meaning. Computation is a process following a well-defined model that is understood and can be expressed in an algorithm, protocol, network topology, etc.

Counter

In typography, a counter is an area entirely or partially enclosed by a letter form or a symbol (the counter-space/ the hole of). Letters containing closed counters include A, B, D, O, P, Q, R, a, b, d, e, g, o, p, and q. Letters containing open counters include c, f, h, i, s etc.

Counter

In typography, a counter is an area entirely or partially enclosed by a letter form or a symbol (the counter-space/ the hole of). Letters containing closed counters include A, B, D, O, P, Q, R, a, b, d, e, g, o, p, and q. Letters containing open counters include c, f, h, i, s etc.

Vector

A vector in computing, specifically when talking about malicious code such as viruses or worms, is the method that this code uses to propagate itself or infect the computer and this sense is similar to, and derived from, its meaning in biology.

Some common vectors:

- buffer overflows -- this is how the Blaster worm was able to propagate
- HTML email with JavaScript or other scripting enhancements
- networking protocol flaws

Channel

Color digital images are made of pixels, and pixels are made of combinations of primary colors. A channel in this context is the grayscale image of the same size as a color image, made of just one of these primary colors. For instance, an image from a standard digital camera will have a red, green and blue channel.

Counting	Counting is the mathematical action of continually adding (or subtracting) one at a time, usually to find out how many objects there are or to set aside a desired number of objects , to find the ordinal number of a particular object, or to find the object with a particular ordinal number. counting is also used (primarily by children) to demonstrate knowledge of the number names and the number system. Sometimes the term counting is used to mean the same as enumeration, i.e. finding the number of elements of a finite set).

Operator	Programming languages generally support a set of operators that are similar to operations in mathematics. A language may contain a fixed number of built-in operators (e.g. + - * = in C and C++), or it may allow the creation of programmer-defined operators (e.g. Haskell). Some programming languages restrict operator symbols to special characters like + or := while others allow also names like `div` (e.g. Pascal).
Kripke structure	A Kripke structure is a type of nondeterministic finite state machine proposed by Saul Kripke in 1963, used in model checking to represent the behaviour of a system. It is basically a graph whose nodes represent the reachable states of the system and whose edges represent state transitions. A labeling function maps each node to a set of properties that hold in the corresponding state.
Asynchronous system	In a synchronous system, operations are coordinated under the centralized control of a fixed-rate clock signal or several clocks. An asynchronous digital system, in contrast, has no global clock: instead, it operates under distributed control, with concurrent hardware components communicating and synchronizing on channels. Modularity Asynchronous systems -- much like object-oriented software -- are typically constructed out of modular 'hardware objects', each with well-defined communication interfaces.
Chord	A chord is a concurrency construct available in Polyphonic C? and Cω inspired by the join pattern of the join-calculus. Synchronicity Cω defines two types of functions synchronous and asynchronous. A synchronous function acts like a standard function in most Object-Oriented Language, upon invocation the function body is executed and a return value may or may not be returned to the caller.
EPSILON	A macro language with high level features including strings and lists, developed by A.P. Ershov at Novosibirsk in 1967. EPSILON was used to implement ALGOL 68 on the M-220 computer.

Protocol	In object-oriented programming, a protocol is what or how unrelated objects use to communicate with each other. These are definitions of methods and values which the objects agree upon in order to cooperate. For example, in Java (where protocols are termed interfaces), the `Comparable` interface specifies a method `compareTo` which implementing classes should implement.

Algorithm

In mathematics and computer science, an algorithm is an effective method expressed as a finite list of well-defined instructions for calculating a function. Algorithms are used for calculation, data processing, and automated reasoning.

Starting from an initial state and initial input (perhaps null), the instructions describe a computation that, when executed, will proceed through a finite number of well-defined successive states, eventually producing "output" and terminating at a final ending state.

Ricart-Agrawala algorithm

The Ricart-Agrawala Algorithm is an algorithm for mutual exclusion on a distributed system. This algorithm is an extension and optimization of Lamport's Distributed Mutual Exclusion Algorithm, by removing the need for release messages. It was developed by Glenn Ricart and Ashok Agrawala.

Dynamics

In music, dynamics normally refers to the volume of a sound or note, but can also refer to every aspect of the execution of a given piece, either stylistic (staccato, legato etc). or functional (velocity). The term is also applied to the written or printed musical notation used to indicate dynamics.

Algorithm

In mathematics and computer science, an algorithm is an effective method expressed as a finite list of well-defined instructions for calculating a function. Algorithms are used for calculation, data processing, and automated reasoning.

Starting from an initial state and initial input (perhaps null), the instructions describe a computation that, when executed, will proceed through a finite number of well-defined successive states, eventually producing "output" and terminating at a final ending state.

Deadlock

A deadlock is a situation where in two or more competing actions are each waiting for the other to finish, and thus neither ever does. It is often seen in a paradox like the "chicken or the egg". The concept of a Catch 22 is similar.

Mutual exclusion	Mutual exclusion algorithms are used in concurrent programming to avoid the simultaneous use of a common resource, such as a global variable, by pieces of computer code called critical sections. A critical section is a piece of code in which a process or thread accesses a common resource. The critical section by itself is not a mechanism or algorithm for mutual exclusion.
Quorum	A quorum is the minimum number of votes that a distributed transaction has to obtain in order to be allowed to perform an operation in a distributed system. A quorum-based technique is implemented to enforce consistent operation in a distributed system. Quorum-based techniques in distributed database systems Quorum-based voting can be used as a replica control method, as well as a commit method to ensure transaction atomicity in the presence of network partitioning.
Protocol	In object-oriented programming, a protocol is what or how unrelated objects use to communicate with each other. These are definitions of methods and values which the objects agree upon in order to cooperate. For example, in Java (where protocols are termed interfaces), the `Comparable` interface specifies a method `compareTo` which implementing classes should implement.

Chapter 10. Deadlock detection in distributed systems

Deadlock	A deadlock is a situation where in two or more competing actions are each waiting for the other to finish, and thus neither ever does. It is often seen in a paradox like the "chicken or the egg". The concept of a Catch 22 is similar.
Algorithm	In mathematics and computer science, an algorithm is an effective method expressed as a finite list of well-defined instructions for calculating a function. Algorithms are used for calculation, data processing, and automated reasoning. Starting from an initial state and initial input (perhaps null), the instructions describe a computation that, when executed, will proceed through a finite number of well-defined successive states, eventually producing "output" and terminating at a final ending state.
Snapshot	In computer systems, a snapshot is the state of a system at a particular point in time. The term was coined as an analogy to that in photography. It can refer to an actual copy of the state of a system or to a capability provided by certain systems.
Resolution	In mathematical logic and automated theorem proving, resolution is a rule of inference leading to a refutation theorem-proving technique for sentences in propositional logic and first-order logic. In other words, iteratively applying the resolution rule in a suitable way allows for telling whether a propositional formula is satisfiable and for proving that a first-order formula is unsatisfiable; this method may prove the satisfiability of a first-order satisfiable formula, but not always, as it is the case for all methods for first-order logic. Resolution was introduced by John Alan Robinson in 1965.
Algorithm	In mathematics and computer science, an algorithm is an effective method expressed as a finite list of well-defined instructions for calculating a function. Algorithms are used for calculation, data processing, and automated reasoning. Starting from an initial state and initial input (perhaps null), the instructions describe a computation that, when executed, will proceed through a finite number of well-defined successive states, eventually producing "output" and terminating at a final ending state.

Computation	Computation is a general term for any type of process, algorithm or measurement; this often includes but is not limited to digital data. This includes phenomena ranging from human thinking to calculations with a more narrow meaning. Computation is a process following a well-defined model that is understood and can be expressed in an algorithm, protocol, network topology, etc.
Computation	Computation is a general term for any type of process, algorithm or measurement; this often includes but is not limited to digital data. This includes phenomena ranging from human thinking to calculations with a more narrow meaning. Computation is a process following a well-defined model that is understood and can be expressed in an algorithm, protocol, network topology, etc.
State	In computer science and automata theory, a state is a unique configuration of information in a program or machine. It is a concept that occasionally extends into some forms of systems programming such as lexers and parsers. Whether the automaton in question is a finite state machine, a pushdown automaton or a full-fledged Turing machine, a state is a particular set of instructions which will be executed in response to the machine's input.
Deadlock	A deadlock is a situation where in two or more competing actions are each waiting for the other to finish, and thus neither ever does. It is often seen in a paradox like the "chicken or the egg". The concept of a Catch 22 is similar.
Tapestry	Tapestry is a distributed hash table which provides a decentralized object location, routing, and multicasting infrastructure for distributed applications. It is composed of a peer-to-peer overlay network offering efficient, scalable, self-repairing, location-aware routing to nearby resources. The first generation of peer-to-peer applications, including Napster, Gnutella, had restricting limitations such as a central directory for Napster and scoped broadcast queries for Gnutella limiting scalability.

Protocol

In object-oriented programming, a protocol is what or how unrelated objects use to communicate with each other. These are definitions of methods and values which the objects agree upon in order to cooperate.

For example, in Java (where protocols are termed interfaces), the `Comparable` interface specifies a method `compareTo` which implementing classes should implement.

State

In computer science and automata theory, a state is a unique configuration of information in a program or machine. It is a concept that occasionally extends into some forms of systems programming such as lexers and parsers.

Whether the automaton in question is a finite state machine, a pushdown automaton or a full-fledged Turing machine, a state is a particular set of instructions which will be executed in response to the machine's input.

Internet

The Internet is a global system of interconnected computer networks that use the standard Internet Protocol Suite (TCP/IP) to serve billions of users worldwide. It is a network of networks that consists of millions of private, public, academic, business, and government networks, of local to global scope, that are linked by a broad array of electronic, wireless and optical networking technologies. The Internet carries a vast range of information resources and services, such as the inter-linked hypertext documents of the World Wide Web (WWW) and the infrastructure to support electronic mail.

Algorithm

In mathematics and computer science, an algorithm is an effective method expressed as a finite list of well-defined instructions for calculating a function. Algorithms are used for calculation, data processing, and automated reasoning.

Starting from an initial state and initial input (perhaps null), the instructions describe a computation that, when executed, will proceed through a finite number of well-defined successive states, eventually producing "output" and terminating at a final ending state.

Password	A password is a secret word or string of characters that is used for authentication, to prove identity or gain access to a resource (example: an access code is a type of password). The password should be kept secret from those not allowed access. The use of passwords is known to be ancient.
Protocol	In object-oriented programming, a protocol is what or how unrelated objects use to communicate with each other. These are definitions of methods and values which the objects agree upon in order to cooperate. For example, in Java (where protocols are termed interfaces), the `Comparable` interface specifies a method `compareTo` which implementing classes should implement.
Shared memory	In computing, shared memory is memory that may be simultaneously accessed by multiple programs with an intent to provide communication among them or avoid redundant copies. Depending on context, programs may run on a single processor or on multiple separate processors. Using memory for communication inside a single program, for example among its multiple threads, is generally not referred to as shared memory.
Consistency	A knowledge base KB is consistent iff its negation is not a tautology. I.e., a knowledge base KB is inconsistent (not consistent) iff there is no interpretation which entails KB. Example of an inconsistent knowledge base: KB := { a, ¬a }

	Consistency in terms of knowledge bases is mostly the same as the natural understanding of consistency.
Algorithm	In mathematics and computer science, an algorithm is an effective method expressed as a finite list of well-defined instructions for calculating a function. Algorithms are used for calculation, data processing, and automated reasoning. Starting from an initial state and initial input (perhaps null), the instructions describe a computation that, when executed, will proceed through a finite number of well-defined successive states, eventually producing "output" and terminating at a final ending state.
Mutual exclusion	Mutual exclusion algorithms are used in concurrent programming to avoid the simultaneous use of a common resource, such as a global variable, by pieces of computer code called critical sections. A critical section is a piece of code in which a process or thread accesses a common resource. The critical section by itself is not a mechanism or algorithm for mutual exclusion.
Snapshot	In computer systems, a snapshot is the state of a system at a particular point in time. The term was coined as an analogy to that in photography. It can refer to an actual copy of the state of a system or to a capability provided by certain systems.

Password	A password is a secret word or string of characters that is used for authentication, to prove identity or gain access to a resource (example: an access code is a type of password). The password should be kept secret from those not allowed access. The use of passwords is known to be ancient.
Protocol	In object-oriented programming, a protocol is what or how unrelated objects use to communicate with each other. These are definitions of methods and values which the objects agree upon in order to cooperate. For example, in Java (where protocols are termed interfaces), the `Comparable` interface specifies a method `compareTo` which implementing classes should implement.
Shared memory	In computing, shared memory is memory that may be simultaneously accessed by multiple programs with an intent to provide communication among them or avoid redundant copies. Depending on context, programs may run on a single processor or on multiple separate processors. Using memory for communication inside a single program, for example among its multiple threads, is generally not referred to as shared memory.
Algorithm	In mathematics and computer science, an algorithm is an effective method expressed as a finite list of well-defined instructions for calculating a function. Algorithms are used for calculation, data processing, and automated reasoning. Starting from an initial state and initial input (perhaps null), the instructions describe a computation that, when executed, will proceed through a finite number of well-defined successive states, eventually producing "output" and terminating at a final ending state.

Rollback

In database technologies, a rollback is an operation which returns the database to some previous state. Rollbacks are important for database integrity, because they mean that the database can be restored to a clean copy even after erroneous operations are performed. They are crucial for recovering from database server crashes; by rolling back any transaction which was active at the time of the crash, the database is restored to a consistent state.

Numbers

Numbers is a spreadsheet application developed by Apple Inc. as part of the iWork productivity suite alongside Keynote and Pages. Numbers 1.0 was announced on August 7, 2007 and thus it is the newest application in the iWork Suite.

Vector

A vector in computing, specifically when talking about malicious code such as viruses or worms, is the method that this code uses to propagate itself or infect the computer and this sense is similar to, and derived from, its meaning in biology.

Some common vectors:

- buffer overflows -- this is how the Blaster worm was able to propagate
- HTML email with JavaScript or other scripting enhancements
- networking protocol flaws

Chapter 14. Consensus and agreement algorithms

Internet	The Internet is a global system of interconnected computer networks that use the standard Internet Protocol Suite (TCP/IP) to serve billions of users worldwide. It is a network of networks that consists of millions of private, public, academic, business, and government networks, of local to global scope, that are linked by a broad array of electronic, wireless and optical networking technologies. The Internet carries a vast range of information resources and services, such as the inter-linked hypertext documents of the World Wide Web (WWW) and the infrastructure to support electronic mail.
Consensus	Consensus is a problem in distributed computing that encapsulates the task of group agreement in the presence of faults. In particular, any process in the group may fail at any time. Consensus is fundamental to core techniques in fault tolerance, such as state machine replication.
Consistency	A knowledge base KB is consistent iff its negation is not a tautology. I.e., a knowledge base KB is inconsistent (not consistent) iff there is no interpretation which entails KB. Example of an inconsistent knowledge base: KB := { a, ¬a } Consistency in terms of knowledge bases is mostly the same as the natural understanding of consistency.
Crash	A crash in computing is a condition where a computer or a program, either an application or part of the operating system, ceases to function properly, often exiting after encountering errors. When a program freezes or hangs, a crash reporting service documents details of the crash. If the program is a critical part of the operating system kernel, the entire computer may crash.

Algorithm

In mathematics and computer science, an algorithm is an effective method expressed as a finite list of well-defined instructions for calculating a function. Algorithms are used for calculation, data processing, and automated reasoning.

Starting from an initial state and initial input (perhaps null), the instructions describe a computation that, when executed, will proceed through a finite number of well-defined successive states, eventually producing "output" and terminating at a final ending state.

Exponential tree

An exponential tree is almost identical to a binary search tree, with the exception that the dimension of the tree is not the same at all levels. In a normal binary search tree, each node has a dimension (d) of 1, and has 2^d children. In an exponential tree, the dimension equals the depth of the node, with the root node having a d = 1. So the second level can hold two nodes, the third can hold eight nodes, the fourth 64 nodes, and so on.

Phase

A Phase in combat is usually a period within a military operation of a longer duration that is a part of a serial chain of logically connected activities planned to culminate in a defined objective or goal.

A phase is usually marked by achievement of significant intermediary objectives, such as tactical within an engagement. A phase may be either limited by time allocated for its execution, or unlimited in time, and defined only by achievement of the objective.

Asynchronous system

In a synchronous system, operations are coordinated under the centralized control of a fixed-rate clock signal or several clocks. An asynchronous digital system, in contrast, has no global clock: instead, it operates under distributed control, with concurrent hardware components communicating and synchronizing on channels.

Modularity

Asynchronous systems -- much like object-oriented software -- are typically constructed out of modular 'hardware objects', each with well-defined communication interfaces.

Terminating Reliable Broadcast	Terminating Reliable Broadcast is a problem in distributed computing that encapsulates the task of broadcasting a message to a set of receiving processes in the presence of faults. In particular, the sender and any other process might fail ("crash") at any time. Problem Description A Terminating Reliable Broadcast protocol typically organizes the system into a sending process and a set of receiving processes, which may include the sender itself.
Commit	In the context of computer science and data management, commit refers to the idea of making a set of tentative changes permanent. A popular usage is at the end of a transaction. A commit is the act of committing.
Shared memory	In computing, shared memory is memory that may be simultaneously accessed by multiple programs with an intent to provide communication among them or avoid redundant copies. Depending on context, programs may run on a single processor or on multiple separate processors. Using memory for communication inside a single program, for example among its multiple threads, is generally not referred to as shared memory.

Chapter 15. Failure detectors

Failure detector	In distributed computing, a failure detector is an application or a subsystem that is responsible for detection of node failures or crashes in a distributed system.
Protocol	In object-oriented programming, a protocol is what or how unrelated objects use to communicate with each other. These are definitions of methods and values which the objects agree upon in order to cooperate. For example, in Java (where protocols are termed interfaces), the `Comparable` interface specifies a method `compareTo` which implementing classes should implement.
Type	In model theory and related areas of mathematics, a type is a set of first-order formulas in a language L with free variables $x_1, x_2, \ldots, x_n$ which are true of a sequence of elements of an L-structure $\mathcal{M}$. Loosely speaking, types describe possible elements of a mathematical structure. Depending on the context, types can be complete or partial and they may use a fixed set of constants, A, from the structure $\mathcal{M}$.
Internet	The Internet is a global system of interconnected computer networks that use the standard Internet Protocol Suite (TCP/IP) to serve billions of users worldwide. It is a network of networks that consists of millions of private, public, academic, business, and government networks, of local to global scope, that are linked by a broad array of electronic, wireless and optical networking technologies. The Internet carries a vast range of information resources and services, such as the inter-linked hypertext documents of the World Wide Web (WWW) and the infrastructure to support electronic mail.
Consensus	Consensus is a problem in distributed computing that encapsulates the task of group agreement in the presence of faults. In particular, any process in the group may fail at any time. Consensus is fundamental to core techniques in fault tolerance, such as state machine replication.

Tapestry

Tapestry is a distributed hash table which provides a decentralized object location, routing, and multicasting infrastructure for distributed applications. It is composed of a peer-to-peer overlay network offering efficient, scalable, self-repairing, location-aware routing to nearby resources.

The first generation of peer-to-peer applications, including Napster, Gnutella, had restricting limitations such as a central directory for Napster and scoped broadcast queries for Gnutella limiting scalability.

Atomic broadcast

In distributed systems, atomic broadcast are received reliably and in the same order by all participants (Défago et al.. 2004).

This problem is usually considered in environments where participants can fail, for example, by crashing.

Order

In scientific classification used in biology, the order is

1. a taxonomic rank used in the classification of organisms. Other well-known ranks are life, domain, kingdom, phylum, class, family, genus, and species, with order fitting in between class and family. An immediately higher rank, superorder, may be added directly above order, while suborder would be a lower rank.
2. a taxonomic unit, a taxon, in that rank.

Property

A property, in some object-oriented programming languages, is a special sort of class member, intermediate between a field (or data member) and a method. Properties are read and written like fields, but property reads and writes are (usually) translated to get and set method calls. The field-like syntax is said to be easier to read and write than lots of method calls, yet the interposition of method calls allows for data validation, active updating (as of GUI visuals), and/or read-only 'fields'.

Chapter 15. Failure detectors

Uniform Consensus

In computer science, Uniform Consensus is a distributed computing problem that is a similar to the consensus problem with one more condition which is no two processes (whether faulty or not) decide differently.

More specifically one should consider this problem:

- Each process has an input, should on decide an output (one-shot problem)
- Uniform Agreement: every two decisions are the same
- Validity: every decision is an input of one of the processes
- Termination: eventually all correct processes decide

.

Implementation

Implementation is the realization of an application, idea, model, design, specification, standard, algorithm, or policy.

In computer science, an implementation(computer science)

· Programming language implementation

· Algorithm

· Application software

· Code

· Computation

· Function

· Method

· Process

· Proceeding

· Procedure

· Scheme

· Solution

· System

· Technique

'.

Relation

In relational model:

A relation is a data structure which consists of a heading and an unordered set of tuples which share the same type.

When Edgar F. Codd invented the relational model, he generalized the concept of binary relation to n-ary relation. Relation is a fundamental concept in relational model.

A relation has zero or more tuples.

A relation value is an instance of a relation.

A relation variable (relvar) is a variable which has a relation value.

In some context, relation means relation variable.

Chapter 16. Authentication in distributed systems

Authentication

Authentication is the act of establishing or confirming something (or someone) as authentic, that is, that claims made by or about the subject are true . This might involve confirming the identity of a person, tracing the origins of an artifact, ensuring that a product is what its packaging and labeling claims to be, or assuring that a computer program is a trusted one.

Authentication methods

In art, antiques, and anthropology, a common problem is verifying that a given artifact was produced by a certain famous person, or was produced in a certain place or period of history.

Protocol

In object-oriented programming, a protocol is what or how unrelated objects use to communicate with each other. These are definitions of methods and values which the objects agree upon in order to cooperate.

For example, in Java (where protocols are termed interfaces), the `Comparable` interface specifies a method `compareTo` which implementing classes should implement.

Snapshot

In computer systems, a snapshot is the state of a system at a particular point in time. The term was coined as an analogy to that in photography. It can refer to an actual copy of the state of a system or to a capability provided by certain systems.

Cryptosystem

There are two different meanings of the word cryptosystem. One is used by the cryptographic community, while the other is the meaning understood by the public.

General meaning

In this meaning, the term cryptosystem is used as shorthand for "cryptographic system".

Authentication server	Authentication servers are servers that provide authentication services to users or other systems via networking. Remotely placed users and other servers authenticate to such a server, and receive cryptographic tickets. These tickets are then exchanged with one another to verify identity.
Server	In computing, the term server is used to refer to one of the following: • a computer program running as a service, to serve the needs or requests of other programs (referred to in this context as "clients") which may or may not be running on the same computer. • a physical computer dedicated to running one or more such services, to serve the needs of programs running on other computers on the same network. • a software/hardware system (i.e. a software service running on a dedicated computer) such as a database server, file server, mail server, or print server. In computer networking, a server is a program that operates as a socket listener. The term server is also often generalized to describe a host that is deployed to execute one or more such programs. A server computer is a computer, or series of computers, that link other computers or electronic devices together.
One-time password	A one-time password is a password that is valid for only one login session or transaction. One time passwords avoid a number of shortcomings that are associated with traditional (static) passwords. The most important shortcoming that is addressed by One time passwords is that, in contrast to static passwords, they are not vulnerable to replay attacks.
Password	A password is a secret word or string of characters that is used for authentication, to prove identity or gain access to a resource (example: an access code is a type of password). The password should be kept secret from those not allowed access. The use of passwords is known to be ancient.

Otway-Rees protocol

The Otway-Rees protocol is a computer network authentication protocol designed for use on insecure networks (eg. the Internet). It allows individuals communicating over such a network to prove their identity to each other while also preventing eavesdropping or replay attacks and allowing for the detection of modification.

Kerberos

Kerberos is a computer network authentication protocol, which allows nodes communicating over a non-secure network to prove their identity to one another in a secure manner. Its designers aimed primarily at a client-server model, and it provides mutual authentication -- both the user and the server verify each other's identity. Kerberos protocol messages are protected against eavesdropping and replay attacks.

Authentication protocol

An authentication protocol is a type of cryptographic protocol with the purpose of authenticating entities wishing to communicate securely.

There are many different authentication protocols such as:

- AKA
- CAVE-based_authentication
- Challenge-handshake authentication protocol
- CRAM-MD5
- Diameter
- Extensible Authentication Protocol
- Host Identity Protocol (HIP)
- Kerberos
- MS-CHAP and MS-CHAPv2 variants of CHAP
- NTLM, also known as NT LAN Manager
- Password-authenticated key agreement protocols
- Password Authentication Protocol
- Protected Extensible Authentication Protocol
- RADIUS
- Secure Remote Password protocol (SRP)
- TACACS and TACACS+
- RFID-Authentication Protocols

Certificate	In computational complexity theory, a certificate is a string that certifies the answer to a computation, or certifies the membership of some string in a language. A certificate is often thought of as a solution path within a verification process, which is used to check whether a problem gives the answer "Yes" or "No". In the decision tree model of computation, certificate complexity is the minimum number of the n input variables of a decision tree that need to be assigned a value in order to definitely establish the value of the Boolean function f.
Public key certificate	In cryptography, a public key certificate is an electronic document which uses a digital signature to bind a public key with an identity -- information such as the name of a person or an organization, their address, and so forth. The certificate can be used to verify that a public key belongs to an individual. In a typical public key infrastructure (PKI) scheme, the signature will be of a certificate authority (CA).
Attack	In computer and computer networks an attack is any attempt to destroy, expose, alter, disable, steal or gain unauthorized access to or make unauthorized use of an asset. Definitions IETF Internet Engineering Task Force defines attack in RFC 2828 as: US Government CNSS Instruction No. 4009 dated 26 April 2010 by Committee on National Security Systems of United States of America defines an attack as:

The increasing dependencies of modern society on information and computers networks (both in private and public sectors, including military) has led to new terms like cyber attack and Cyberwarfare.

CNSS Instruction No. 4009 define a cyber attack as:

Phenomenology

An attack can be active or passive.

An attack can be perpetrated by an insider or from outside the organization;

> An "inside attack" is an attack initiated by an entity inside the security perimeter (an "insider"), i.e., an entity that is authorized to access system resources but uses them in a way not approved by those who granted the authorization.
> An "outside attack" is initiated from outside the perimeter, by an unauthorized or illegitimate user of the system (an "outsider").

Layer

In object-oriented design, a layer is a group of classes that have the same set of link-time module dependencies to other modules. In other words, a layer is a group of reusable components that are reusable in similar circumstances. In programming languages, the layer distinction is often expressed as "import" dependencies between software modules.

Dictionaries

A dictionary is a collection of words in a specific language, often listed alphabetically, with usage information, definitions, etymologies, phonetics, pronunciations, and other information; or a book of words in one language with their equivalents in another, also known as a lexicon. According to Nielsen 2008 a dictionary may be regarded as a lexicographical product that is characterised by three significant features: (1) it has been prepared for one or more functions; (2) it contains data that have been selected for the purpose of fulfilling those functions; and (3) its lexicographic structures link and establish relationships between the data so that they can meet the needs of users and fulfil the functions of the dictionary.

In many languages, words can appear in many different forms, but only the undeclined or unconjugated form appears as the headword in most dictionaries.

Dictionary attack	In cryptanalysis and computer security, a dictionary attack is a technique for defeating a cipher or authentication mechanism by trying to determine its decryption key or passphrase by searching likely possibilities. A dictionary attack uses a targeted technique of successively trying all the words in an exhaustive list called a dictionary (from a pre-arranged list of values). In contrast with a brute force attack, where a large proportion key space is searched systematically, a dictionary attack tries only those possibilities which are most likely to succeed, typically derived from a list of words for example a dictionary (hence the phrase dictionary attack) or a bible etc.
Secure Remote Password protocol	The Secure Remote Password protocol is a password-authenticated key agreement protocol. Overview The SRP protocol has a number of desirable properties: it allows a user to authenticate himself to a server, it is resistant to dictionary attacks mounted by an eavesdropper, and it does not require a trusted third party. It effectively conveys a zero-knowledge password proof from the user to the server.

Chapter 17. Self-stabilization

Chord

A chord is a concurrency construct available in Polyphonic C? and Cω inspired by the join pattern of the join-calculus.

Synchronicity

Cω defines two types of functions synchronous and asynchronous. A synchronous function acts like a standard function in most Object-Oriented Language, upon invocation the function body is executed and a return value may or may not be returned to the caller.

Password

A password is a secret word or string of characters that is used for authentication, to prove identity or gain access to a resource (example: an access code is a type of password). The password should be kept secret from those not allowed access.

The use of passwords is known to be ancient.

Closure

In computer science, a closure is a first-class function with free variables that are bound in the lexical environment. Such a function is said to be "closed over" its free variables. A closure is defined within the scope of its free variables, and the extent of those variables is at least as long as the lifetime of the closure itself.

Convergence

Precisely every individual in the population is identical. While full convergence might be seen in genetic algorithms using only cross over, such convergence is seldom seen in genetic programming using Koza's subtree swapping crossover. However, populations often stabilise after a time, in the sense that the best programs all have a common ancestor and their behaviour is very similar (or identical) both to each other and to that of high fitness programs from the previous (and future?) generations.

Protocol

In object-oriented programming, a protocol is what or how unrelated objects use to communicate with each other. These are definitions of methods and values which the objects agree upon in order to cooperate.

For example, in Java (where protocols are termed interfaces), the `Comparable` interface specifies a method `compareTo` which implementing classes should implement.

Relation

In relational model:

> A relation is a data structure which consists of a heading and an unordered set of tuples which share the same type.
>
> > When Edgar F. Codd invented the relational model, he generalized the concept of binary relation to n-ary relation. Relation is a fundamental concept in relational model.
>
> A relation has zero or more tuples.
> A relation value is an instance of a relation.
> A relation variable (relvar) is a variable which has a relation value.

In some context, relation means relation variable.

Self-stabilization

Self-stabilization is a concept of fault-tolerance in distributed computing. A distributed system that is self-stabilizing will end up in a correct state no matter what state it is initialized with. That correct state is reached after a finite number of execution steps.

Snapshot

In computer systems, a snapshot is the state of a system at a particular point in time. The term was coined as an analogy to that in photography. It can refer to an actual copy of the state of a system or to a capability provided by certain systems.

State

In computer science and automata theory, a state is a unique configuration of information in a program or machine. It is a concept that occasionally extends into some forms of systems programming such as lexers and parsers.

Whether the automaton in question is a finite state machine, a pushdown automaton or a full-fledged Turing machine, a state is a particular set of instructions which will be executed in response to the machine's input.

Transient

Java

In the Java programming language, `transient` is a keyword used as a field modifier. When a field is declared transient, it would not be serialized even if the class to which it belongs is serialized. In Java, methods, classes and interfaces cannot be declared as transient.

Tapestry

Tapestry is a distributed hash table which provides a decentralized object location, routing, and multicasting infrastructure for distributed applications. It is composed of a peer-to-peer overlay network offering efficient, scalable, self-repairing, location-aware routing to nearby resources.

The first generation of peer-to-peer applications, including Napster, Gnutella, had restricting limitations such as a central directory for Napster and scoped broadcast queries for Gnutella limiting scalability.

Topology

In chemistry, topology provides a convenient way of describing and predicting the molecular structure within the constraints of three-dimensional (3-D) space. Given the determinants of chemical bonding and the chemical properties of the atoms, topology provides a model for explaining how the atoms ethereal wave functions must fit together. Molecular topology is a part of mathematical chemistry dealing with the algebraic description of chemical compounds so allowing an unique and easy characterization of them.

Spanning tree

In the mathematical field of graph theory, a spanning tree T of a connected, undirected graph G is a tree composed of all the vertices and some (or perhaps all) of the edges of G. Informally, a spanning tree of G is a selection of edges of G that form a tree spanning every vertex. That is, every vertex lies in the tree, but no cycles (or loops) are formed. On the other hand, every bridge of G must belong to T.

A spanning tree of a connected graph G can also be defined as a maximal set of edges of G that contains no cycle, or as a minimal set of edges that connect all vertices.

Chapter 17. Self-stabilization

Algorithm	In mathematics and computer science, an algorithm is an effective method expressed as a finite list of well-defined instructions for calculating a function. Algorithms are used for calculation, data processing, and automated reasoning. Starting from an initial state and initial input (perhaps null), the instructions describe a computation that, when executed, will proceed through a finite number of well-defined successive states, eventually producing "output" and terminating at a final ending state.
Independent set	In graph theory, an independent set is a set of vertices in a graph, no two of which are adjacent. That is, it is a set I of vertices such that for every two vertices in I, there is no edge connecting the two. Equivalently, each edge in the graph has at most one endpoint in I. The size of an independent set is the number of vertices it contains.
Compiler	A compiler is a computer program (or set of programs) that transforms source code written in a programming language (the source language) into another computer language (the target language, often having a binary form known as object code). The most common reason for wanting to transform source code is to create an executable program. The name "compiler" is primarily used for programs that translate source code from a high-level programming language to a lower level language (e.g., assembly language or machine code).
Fault	In document ISO/CD 10303-226, a fault is defined as an abnormal condition or defect at the component, equipment, or sub-system level which may lead to a failure.

According to the Federal Standard 1037C of the United States, the term fault has the following meanings:

1. An accidental condition that causes a functional unit to fail to perform its required function.
2. A defect that causes a reproducible or catastrophic malfunction. A malfunction is considered reproducible if it occurs consistently under the same circumstances.
3. In power systems, an unintentional short-circuit, or partial short-circuit, between energized conductors or between an energized conductor and ground.

Napster

Napster was an online music peer-to-peer file sharing service created by Shawn Fanning while he was attending Northeastern University in Boston. The service operated between June 1999 and July 2001. Its technology allowed people to easily share their MP3 files with other participants, bypassing the established market for such songs and thus leading to massive copyright violations of music and film media as well as other intellectual property.

Although the original service was shut down by court order, it paved the way for decentralized peer-to-peer file distribution programs, which have been much harder to control.

Otway-Rees protocol

The Otway-Rees protocol is a computer network authentication protocol designed for use on insecure networks (eg. the Internet). It allows individuals communicating over such a network to prove their identity to each other while also preventing eavesdropping or replay attacks and allowing for the detection of modification.

Interconnection

In telecommunications, interconnection is the physical linking of a carrier's network with equipment or facilities not belonging to that network. The term may refer to a connection between a carrier's facilities and the equipment belonging to its customer, or to a connection between two (or more) carriers.

In United States regulatory law, interconnection is specifically defined (47 C.F.R. 51.5) as "the linking of two networks for the mutual exchange of traffic."

One of the primary tools used by regulators to introduce competition in telecommunications markets has been to impose interconnection requirements on dominant carriers.

Protocol

In object-oriented programming, a protocol is what or how unrelated objects use to communicate with each other. These are definitions of methods and values which the objects agree upon in order to cooperate.

For example, in Java (where protocols are termed interfaces), the `Comparable` interface specifies a method `compareTo` which implementing classes should implement.

Snapshot

In computer systems, a snapshot is the state of a system at a particular point in time. The term was coined as an analogy to that in photography. It can refer to an actual copy of the state of a system or to a capability provided by certain systems.

Gnutella

Gnutella is a large peer-to-peer network which, at the time of its creation, was the first decentralized peer-to-peer network of its kind, leading to other, later networks adopting the model. It celebrated a decade of existence on March 14, 2010 and has a user base in the millions for peer-to-peer file sharing.

In June 2005, Gnutella's population was 1.81 million computers increasing to over three million nodes by January 2006. In late 2007, it was the most popular file sharing network on the Internet with an estimated market share of more than 40%.

Peer-to-peer

Peer-to-peer computing or networking is a distributed application architecture that partitions tasks or work loads between peers. Peers are equally privileged, equipotent participants in the application. They are said to form a peer-to-peer network of nodes.

Replication

Replication is the process of sharing information so as to ensure consistency between redundant resources, such as software or hardware components, to improve reliability, fault-tolerance, or accessibility. It could be data replication if the same data is stored on multiple storage devices, or computation replication if the same computing task is executed many times. A computational task is typically replicated in space, i.e. executed on separate devices, or it could be replicated in time, if it is executed repeatedly on a single device.

Chord

A chord is a concurrency construct available in Polyphonic C? and Cω inspired by the join pattern of the join-calculus.

Synchronicity

Cω defines two types of functions synchronous and asynchronous. A synchronous function acts like a standard function in most Object-Oriented Language, upon invocation the function body is executed and a return value may or may not be returned to the caller.

Tapestry

Tapestry is a distributed hash table which provides a decentralized object location, routing, and multicasting infrastructure for distributed applications. It is composed of a peer-to-peer overlay network offering efficient, scalable, self-repairing, location-aware routing to nearby resources.

The first generation of peer-to-peer applications, including Napster, Gnutella, had restricting limitations such as a central directory for Napster and scoped broadcast queries for Gnutella limiting scalability.

Algorithm

In mathematics and computer science, an algorithm is an effective method expressed as a finite list of well-defined instructions for calculating a function. Algorithms are used for calculation, data processing, and automated reasoning.

Starting from an initial state and initial input (perhaps null), the instructions describe a computation that, when executed, will proceed through a finite number of well-defined successive states, eventually producing "output" and terminating at a final ending state.

Internet

The Internet is a global system of interconnected computer networks that use the standard Internet Protocol Suite (TCP/IP) to serve billions of users worldwide. It is a network of networks that consists of millions of private, public, academic, business, and government networks, of local to global scope, that are linked by a broad array of electronic, wireless and optical networking technologies. The Internet carries a vast range of information resources and services, such as the inter-linked hypertext documents of the World Wide Web (WWW) and the infrastructure to support electronic mail.

Attack

In computer and computer networks an attack is any attempt to destroy, expose, alter, disable, steal or gain unauthorized access to or make unauthorized use of an asset.

Definitions

IETF

Internet Engineering Task Force defines attack in RFC 2828 as:

US Government

CNSS Instruction No. 4009 dated 26 April 2010 by Committee on National Security Systems of United States of America defines an attack as:

The increasing dependencies of modern society on information and computers networks (both in private and public sectors, including military) has led to new terms like cyber attack and Cyberwarfare.

CNSS Instruction No. 4009 define a cyber attack as:

Phenomenology

An attack can be active or passive.

An attack can be perpetrated by an insider or from outside the organization;

> An "inside attack" is an attack initiated by an entity inside the security perimeter (an "insider"), i.e., an entity that is authorized to access system resources but uses them in a way not approved by those who granted the authorization.
> An "outside attack" is initiated from outside the perimeter, by an unauthorized or illegitimate user of the system (an "outsider").

CPSIA information can be obtained
at www.ICGtesting.com
Printed in the USA
LVOW09s1607070217
523494LV00002B/49/P